T0197117

# FIGHTING
## SADDAM IN IRAQ
## AND ISIS IN SYRIA

## STEVEN GONZALEZ

# FIGHTING SADDAM IN IRAQ AND ISIS IN SYRIA

iUniverse books may be ordered through booksellers or by contacting:

iUniverse
1663 Liberty Drive
Bloomington, IN 47403
www.iuniverse.com
1-800-Authors (1-800-288-4677)

ISBN: 978-1-5320-2863-2 (sc)
ISBN: 978-1-5320-2862-5 (e)

Library of Congress Control Number: 2017911163

Print information available on the last page.

iUniverse rev. date: 08/04/2017

# ACKNOWLEDGMENTS

I lost three great friends and fighters in the fight against ISIS: Mario Nunes from Portugal, Jamie Bright from Australia, and S. Ariel from Iran.

I miss them, and I miss their great smiles.

# MY START

In March 2003, I was a Sergeant First Class. I was serving with the Army Reserve Unit in the 302$^{nd}$ Military Police Company based in Fort Worth, Texas. I was also a police officer for the Haltom City Police Department in Haltom City, Texas.

On this date, the unit and I were currently at Camp Arifjan, Kuwait, waiting for the attack order on Iraq. President George W. Bush's administration stated that Iraq's president, Saddam Hussein, did in fact have weapons of mass destruction. This made Bush's case for the war on Iraq to remove Saddam Hussein.

Camp Arifjan was one of the staging military points, and there were 20,000 troops stationed there from the United States, the United Kingdom, Spain, Poland, and Australia. Saddam Hussein's military forces did fire scud missiles at us, and we were informed that the missiles may have contained chemicals. As a result, we had to work, eat, sleep, and fight with full MOPP gear and gas masks. The US military response was to set up Patriot batteries where we were stationed as well as throughout Kuwait. The Patriot batteries did have a high success rate in shooting down Saddam's missiles.

SFC Edward Davis and I were promoted back at Fort Hood, Texas. This is where all the processing and training would begin. Both SFC Davis and I were ordered to work in the 302$^{nd}$ Company Tactical Operation Center (TOC).

While at Camp Arifjan, our company received orders to move to Camp Wolf, which was another staging camp on the grounds of the Kuwait International Airport. While on smoke breaks, I watched both military and civilian aircraft land and take off. Our company was tasked with escorting convoys to other staging points along the Kuwait and Iraq border.

On March 20, the attack order was given, and we invaded Iraq. The first Iraqi town we overran was Safwan, which is where the cease-fire negotiations between General Norman Schwarzkopf and Iraqi General Sultan Hashim Ahmad took place in the 1991 Persian Gulf War. There were oil rigs in the area, and the Iraqi Army lit them on fire as it fled from the Kuwait border.

The British military was ordered to attack the Iraqi city of Basra and the sea port city of Umm Qasr. The British military assigned its own military police force in Safwan, and we were attached to them. Our company received orders, and our missions took place around the Safwan area. Our main missions were escorting convoys from CSC Navistar in Kuwait, which we first started and formed. This area is still very much used by both Iraqi and Kuwaiti people as a trading post today.

The U.S. military built and opened Camp Bucca, which was between Safwan and Umm Qasr, as a prisoner of war camp. The

Iraqi POWs were processed and detained here during the first stages of the war. We would drive by in our Humvees en route from Safwan to Umm Qasr. From time to time, I remember seeing the POWs standing outside tents. On March 23, 2003, the Iraqi military ambushed a US Army unit, the 507th Maintenance Company, in the Iraqi city of Nasiriyah and took several American POWs. One of our own company lieutenants came into our tent, where we set up headquarters, and gave us the news. I remember hitting the table with my hand and saying, "Damn, our first American POWs of the war."

Our company received orders to relocate to Tallil Air Base, a U.S. Air Force Base near Nasiriyah, Iraq. We had to cross the Euphrates River to get from one base to the other.

We would spend our last six months here. All units had to spend twelve months with boots on ground before they could return home. Our main mission was as convoy escorts, but we also set up checkpoints and provided security around the air base perimeter.

On November 12, 2003, the Italian Military Police was based at the air base, and it had set up its headquarters building in town. It was tasked with training the Iraqi police. Insurgents fired at the Iraqi police checkpoint on the main road to the Italian headquarters. The Iraqi police returned fire, couldn't stop the attack, but did kill some insurgents, which slowed the truck they were in. After the police scattered, the insurgents moved the roadblock. A tanker truck rigged with explosives detonated next to the three-story building. At that time, I was playing cards with SPC Julian Hernandez on his cot. We felt the ground shake, ran out of the tent, and saw a big cloud of smoke coming from town. At least twenty-eight people were killed, and more than a hundred were injured. Among these, four Italian Army soldiers were killed, and thirteen Italians MPs were killed. Our unit did provide an honor guard when the Italians were flown home.

On July 22, 2003, the US military received a tip that Saddam's sons, Uday and Qusay Hussein, were staying in a house in Mosul, Iraq. The US military surrounded the house and confirmed that both sons were there. A four-hour gun battle ensued in which both sons were killed.

On December 13, 2003, after spending nine months on the run, a US task force captured Saddam Hussein in Ad-Dawr, Iraq. The task force's job during the war was to find or kill Saddam Hussein. He was found hiding in a small, walled, mud hut compound—a spider hole—which I am sure was a far cry from usual for him since he had thirty palaces built for himself. Once he was pulled from the spider hole, he stated, "I am Saddam Hussein, president of Iraq, and I want to negotiate."

After I served that first year in the Iraq War, Saddam, his whole administration, and his sons were removed from power. As Iraq became very unstable, we did witness lots of crime and looting. The facts are that Saddam attacked Iran, and a war occurred from 1980 to 1988. On March 16, 1988, Saddam used chemical gas on the Kurdish people in northern Iraq. In August 1990, Saddam attacked Kuwait, and in 1991, during the Persian Gulf War, Saddam did fire thirty-nine scud missiles at Israel. So, in my own personal view, we had just removed the biggest bully on the block. I am very glad that I spent that year helping the Shia Muslim people.

Abu Bakr al-Baghdadi was born in Iraq, and he would form ISIS and become the group's leader. On February 2, 2004, the U.S. military arrested al-Baghdadi near Fallujah, Iraq and sent him to the Camp Bucca detention center. At this point, ISIS did not yet exist, and it would be years before he formed ISIS. In December 2004, he was released as a POW. Abu Bakr al-Baghdadi was back at Camp Bucca in 2005 and 2009. During these times, he was imprisoned with other future leaders of ISIS.

# MY NEXT CHAPTER: THE IRAQI POLICE

On March 2004, our company received orders to return home to Texas. Once we got back to Fort Hood, we were processed and debriefed on our overseas tour. We were then sent back to our home unit in Grand Prairie, Texas. There were a few more days of processing, and then we were released from the unit. I returned to work with the Haltom City Police Department, and it felt great to be back on patrol. The city officials of Haltom City thanked me for the year I served in Iraq. They honored me with a welcome-home event in one of the city parks. The event made the news, and I received a plaque from the mayor of Haltom City. Channel 8, an ABC affiliate, aired the story on its evening news.

In 2005, I retired after serving twenty-one years in the military. I received a great retirement party in downtown Fort Worth with some fellow military personnel and close friends. I did observe that our military was still in Iraq. I remember thinking about what I could do to help get our people back home. A friend informed me about a position with DynCorp International. The most important requirement for this position was to train the Iraqi police. In 2007 and 2008, I went back to Iraq to help train the Iraqi police. As part of DynCorp, we did go to Virginia to do some processing and training. We then went to Fort Bliss, Texas, and from there, we flew back to the Middle East.

In March 2007, we flew into Kuwait, and there were forty-four of us in our group. We were called international police advisors (IPAs). We then flew into Baghdad and were bused to Camp Striker and forprocessing. We were informed that we needed to get into groups of four, and then we would be scattered around the county. For our group, it was Wayne Cunningham, Jody Bergholm, both of South Carolina, Craig Hammer, and me. We were informed that we would be sent to the Anbar Province, west of Baghdad. We were informed that there was still a lot of shooting going on there—it was like the Wild West out there. Each group was given one computer to use, so our daily reports could be filled out, and sent in, if possible. Our US Marines were in charge of this area of operation. Groups of Marines were trained just for this task, and they were called police transitional teams (PTTs). The IPAs and PTTs trained the Iraqi police (IP).

We boarded a C-17 plane, which had plenty of seats, and we flew to Al Asad air base. We spent a few days there, and the Marines flew us to Al-Qaim, Iraq, in a CH-53. The CH-53 was in poor working condition, and oil dripped down from the overhead motor blade. When we got to Al-Qaim, we and our bags were covered in oil. A Marine inside said, "Welcome to Iraq."

Our camp commander, Axel Reyes, was from California. He picked us up and took us to his office. There was a map on the wall, and he showed us where Al-Qaim was, which was along the Euphrates River and the Syrian border. He pointed to the town of

Ar-Rutbah, south of Al-Qaim, and he said the PTT needed IPAs and that the four of us would be going. We were briefed that instead of staying at FOB or COB, we would be working, training, and living with the IP. We said, "Yes, sir," and grabbed our bags. Jody and Wayne flew out first. They made it, but they did not come back. Due to sandstorms in the area, Craig and I couldn't fly out for a few weeks; finally, we flew on CH-47 Chinook helicopter to Ar-Rutbah.

Craig and I landed at FOB: Korean Village (KV), and we found the building that belonged to our PTT guys, but they were not there, nor were Jody or Wayne. Craig and I walked around the post, and we found the chow hall, laundry building, barber shop, PX, showers, and the recreational hall which had a television, pool table, and online access. There was always a long line to use the Internet. You got fifteen minuteson the computer, and then you had to get back into line. Craig and I stayed at KV for a few days. A Marine then told us he was with the PTT and that he was going to take us to Ar-Rutbah to join up with everyone else. Craig and I loaded our bags in the Humvees, and we were off for the three-hour road trip.

Once Craig and I were in Ar-Rutbah, with a population of 22,000, we pulled into one of the city buildings where everyone else was staying. We got to meet our PTT-21 counterparts, and we did meet back up with Jody and Wayne. Our team picked Wayne to be our officer in charge (OIC). The PTT briefed us that there were no IPs in town, but they would be sent for once they graduated from the police academy in Bagdad. The new police headquarters building was to be ready soon, and a police colonel and his administration would be arriving to take over responsibility of the police building and the city. We were also responsible for all of the IPs in two other towns, Akashat, population 5,000, and Al Walid, population 1,000. The PTT said that all of the IPs in all three towns would be paid in cash once a month, and the money had to be counted by hand before each payday. Each PTT had interpreters assigned with them, and they helped us greatly while working with the IPs and Iraqi communities.

The history behind our IP's new police headquarters building was that the British had built the fort in the 1930s. That was when Iraq became independent from the British, and the British called it Rutbah Wells Fort. The insurgents blew two holes in it, the Iraqis patched it up, and we moved in with no power at first. Craig, Jody, Wayne, and I would live for a full year in the fort as we worked with the IPs and the communities of Ar-Rubah, Akashat, and Walid. The four of us actually shared a room, and we had two sets of bunk beds and one desk.

We did get our new police chief and his staff in, and the Marines, in a CH-53, flew in on the other side of town. Our first group of new police recruits got settled in the fort with no problems. We met with the chief and his staff, and we all agreed that our main goals were to establish a proactive police department, enforce law and order, and protect each citizen of the community. We were informed that when Saddam was in power, the police sat at the station, and the citizens had to go to the station to file a complaint. It was established that the IPs would conduct three foot patrols a day and shake hands with citizens in the neighborhoods and businesses. Each IP was issued an AK-47 and a Glock pistol, and we conducted guard mounts to make sure they had them before going on duty. We were told that there were twenty new police trucks at KV, and we got as many of the IPs to drive them back to Ar-Rutbah, so that the IPs could conduct mobile patrols. Even though the IPs got new police trucks, we still conducted the three foot patrols to stay as proactive as possible, and we did the same for the communities in Akahat and Walid.

The police chief met with other city officials to ensure that the police force provided for the safety of the city and community. With help from our interpreter, we conducted ongoing training classes with the IPs in the training room. We assigned two IP officers to become training officers so that in the future they could conduct training classes on their own. A jail was established in the fort, and when the IPs arrested someone and put the prisoner inside the jail, the IPs would ensure the prisoner was fed three meals a day and not beaten for any reason. With help from our interpreter, we conducted a jail check every hour to ensure no human rights violations were being conducted inside the jail. We conducted the same jail checks procedures at the IP jails in Akashat and Walid.

As time went on, we got to know the IPs better, and we became friends. The IP who drove for the chief we called Cowboy, and he was from Al- Qaim. We decided to have an open house at the police department, so any citizens and kids could see the police station and police trucks. Cowboy and I cleaned and washed one of the police trucks, so it would be clean for the kids.

For the three foot patrols, one was set for two hours, one was set for three hours, and the last was set for two hours, and they started to take their toll on my feet and the soles on my boots, which I had to replace a few times. One night at ten, an IED went off in front of the fort. Everyone ran to see what happened and took cover. Cowboy and I went to the top of the fort, and we all watched to make sure no one was attacked. It was three the next morning when the all-clear signal was given. It looked like whoever set the IED off was determined to kill us as we went on our foot patrols.

When we were first in Al-Qaim, the Marines issued Craig, Jody, Wayne, and me Marine uniforms so that we would blend in with the rest of the Marines. We did set up a firing range, in Ar-Rutbah, so the IPs could practice from time to time. Some IPs brought to our attention that they had heard that there were some 155-mm rounds, which could be used for IEDs, in the desert away from the city. We all got into our Humvees and police trucks, and the IPs drove to the spot. They started digging and uncovered eleven rounds. We called the EOD team, and it safely blew up the rounds.No one was hurt or killed. Major General Walter Gaskin came out to the fort to meet with our PTT and assess how the mission was going. He was the commanding Marine general in the Anbar Province area. Our six-month PTT tour was over, and we said our goodbyes. A new PTT replaced us.

# TIME AWAY AND BACK TO WORK

Back at KV, I checked my email and saw that my vacation had been approved by our administration. The Marines flew me on CH-47 helicopters from KV to Al-Asad, to Baghdad, and then to Camp Klecker. I flew from Baghdad to Amman, Jordan. I stayed at the Sheraton Hotel, where I got a shower and change of clothes. I have a domestic partner, Anthony Marquez, and we have been together since 1993. He wanted to meet in Paris, and that is where we met up. We walked around the city, saw the Eiffel Tower, and took in lots of the sights. We then caught the bullet train to Belgium, the Netherlands, Germany, the Czech Republic, Austria, Italy, and Switzerland. We did make it back to Paris, and we both had a great time traveling around Europe. Anthony headed back to Texas, and I headed back to Iraq.

I made it back to Ar-Rutbah, and I met our new PTT guys. Craig, Jody, Wayne and I all got back to work. We decided to make road trips to Akashat and Walid, and it took three hours to get to Akashat, and it took four hours to Walid. We did not take IPs with us, for they had to stay in Ar-Rutbah. All the PTTs, IPAs, and interpreters loaded up in the Humvees and hit the road. We did have to get up on Highway 1, which is like any other highway, and we stayed very vigilant until we got to our destinations. We turned on Road 20, and once we got to Akashat, we made contact with the police chief to see how things were going and if he needed any help. I did a thirty-minute training class with the IPs, and we then checked the jail for any human rights violations. We loaded up in the Humvees and headed to Walid. We turned back to Highway 1 and turned on Road 11, and we were in Walid. Walid is a main crossing point from Iraq into Syria, so they stayed very busy here. We made contact with the chief to see how things were going and whether he needed any help. Again, I conducted a thirty-minute training class with the IPs and checked the jail for any human rights violations. This was how each road trip went when we checked on the IPs and both towns, and then we would head back to Ar-Rutbah.

Craig's, Jody's, Wayne's, and my year marks were up, and within that year, we formed the Al-Rutbah police force from the ground up. It became a fully functioning police force. When I was at KV, an Army guy knocked at our door and explained that he was tasked with the Iraqi highway patrol. He asked if I could help him, and I told him I could. Since the highway patrol patrolled on Highway 1 and some back roads, I told them to stop in with the IPs in Al-Rutbah and to meet with the chief to exchange any intelligence they may have. I also told him to do the same for the IPs in Akashat and Walid. I did see them a few times doing that, and I saw them park their Iraqi highway patrol trucks in the back of the fort. Wayne and Jody decided to head back home, and Craig and I decided to do another year. Craig was sent to another town. I was still alive, so I did another year, and I was asked if I could go to Akashat for thirty days to train a new IPA there. I was then to report to Al-Qaim. I said, "Yes, sir." As the four of us IPAs spent our last days in Ar-Rutbah, the new IPA guys showed up to relieve us. We briefed them and gave them the keys to the fort.

I arrived in Akasat and met with the new IPA assigned there. I also met with the Army PTT, who was issued new armored vehicles. I advised them that I could show them the process with the IPs and chief, and our interpreter, Omar, went with us. We all went to the police station, and I introduced everyone to the chief and IPs assigned there. We conducted many foot patrols in the neighborhood and business area of the town. We also held many training classes with the IPs and checked the jail for any human rights violations. There was a train track that ran next to the town, and it went somewhere in Syria. I did see several trains still using the track, and this happened in both the day and night. My thirty days ended, and the Marines flew me on an Osprey helicopter from KV to Al-Qaim.

When I got to Al-Qaim, which is along the Euphrates River, we were set up at Camp Gannon, and I met with the new Marines PTT-7. They were issued new MRAP vehicles, which were much bigger than the Humvees, and the air conditioning worked great in them. The two IPAs I was to be working with were Mike Langland of Missouri and Robert Hensley of Washington. We were assigned to police headquarters, as was our interpreter. From the back of Camp Gannon, you could clearly see the no-man's zone and then into Syria. I remember thinking that Syria sure was quiet. We all traveled to the police station, and I saw Cowboy., who had just spent a year at the fort in Al-Rutbah., He was from Al-Qaim when he was transferred to this police station. It was great seeing him again.

Al-Qaim's population was over 150,000, and there was a cement plant there, which I remember seeing when we were out on the road. The city was alive with people. When we helped the IPs on checkpoints downtown, we would see plenty of stores and bazaars with many goats walking around. It was great to see the kids in school getting an education. I do remember getting care packages from the US with notes asking us to deliver school supplies to the kids in school. That is what we did, and the kids got new school supplies and backpacks. There was a good working hospital and medical staff as well as a fire department with great first-responder personnel.

The police chief was doing a great job with the station and the IPs as well as the community. The IPs did make quite a few arrests, so there was always some prisoner in the jail, and we did our jail checks to ensure no human rights violations were happening. With the help of our interpreter, we conducted training classes with the IPs. There was a joint communication center (JCC) building there. Two Marines and one Iraqi Army soldier were posted there, and I did help them out from time to time. We did take the IPs out to the gun range, and they did great. When we were at the police station, I did observe that they had some nice police trucks, cars, and motorcycles with which to conduct their patrols around the community. There were two substations around, in Romanah and Sadah, and we did make it to them several times to check on the IPs posted there. When I was at Camp Gannon, on the way to the chow hall, I would occasionally see a military trailer with a big gun boat on it, but I never saw them put in on the Euphrates River, which was right there.

After about six months, I was going on my last vacation, and I decided I would stay in Amman, Jordan, to get some Holy Land sightseeing in. I had a friend, SSG Max Hall, in Fallujah, and I told him I was going to visit with him before I left for Baghdad. The Marines flew me on an Osprey from Camp Gannon to Fallujah; the Marines were still firing their M-198 Howitzer, outbound rounds. Max and I were together, in 2003, for the main push into Baghdad. Now he was with the Army 812th Military Police Company, and it was great to see him again. We were able to get a few days of visiting in. The Marines did fly me onto Baghdad, and I caught a flight to Amman. I stayed at the Sheraton, and I hired a local guide to take me around to the Holy Land sights. I went to Petra, the Dead Sea, the Jordan River (where Jesus was baptized), Mount Nebo, and where Moses put up the Brazen Serpent. My guide even set it up, and I went to Jerusalem, Israel, and I stood in the spot where Jesus was crucified. I spent a few days there. I had to go through a lot of checkpoints, in both Israel and Jordan, as I headed back to Amman. After spending twenty-eight days in the Holy Land, I headed back to Camp Gannon to get back to work.

I got sent to Rawah, population 13,900, to help IPA Chris Holland. The Marines flew me by Osprey to Rawah. Chris and a PTT-20 picked me up from the COB, and we had to cross the Rawah Bridge to get across the Euphrates River and into town. Chris showed me around. The police station is pretty well-established, and we did meet with the chief. The 3rd Battalion 2nd Marines (3/2) is an infantry battalion, with 1,000 Marines and sailors, who were also posted at the police compound. Needless to say, we did 10,000 foot patrols with the 3/2 guys and IPs.

I did get up at seven each morning while posted there to make the IP guard mount an hour later. The captain would conduct it, I would get up front and give a pep talk, and I would then send them off for duty. We conducted our foot patrols, and with the 3/2 guys, our line was pretty long. The PTT conducted a lot of classes with the IPs, and I remember our doc gave great medical classes. The IPAs, PTT, and interpreter would have nightly meetings to go over what we could teach the IPs the next day. While in the building one day, we heard an explosion, and the ground shook. We all put on our gear and ran for the roof, and we heard on the radio that someone planted an IED in front of the police station and set it off. No one had been injured or killed, the 3/2 guys cleared it, and we all went back to work. A few weeks later, we were instructed to go to Anah, population 27,211, and help with the IPs posted there. We all arrived in Anah and met with the police chief and the IPs. We all saw that the station was very well-established, and we checked on the jail for any human rights violations. We headed back to Rawah for a grilled dinner, which, thank God, the PTT loved doing every night.

I received instruction that they were sending another IPA, Chris Dudley, to relieve me, and I was to report to Camp Mesa at Al Asad. Chris did relieve me; I showed him the police station and introduced him to the police chief and IPs. The PTT drove me to Al Asad, as we turned south onto Road 12, and they dropped me off at Camp Mesa. I checked in with our camp commander, and he asked me if I would mind being posted at Khan al Baghdadi. I told him, "No, sir." I grabbed my bags and moved into Camp Mesa. Al Asad had four chow halls we could go eat at as well as a very big PX.

I did meet with the two IPAs, PTT-2, who were issued the MRAP vehicles, and our interpreter, and they were already posted with Baghdadi, population 5,000. We went to the police station and met with the chief and IPs, and the building seemed to be empty upon our arrival. The town people were always busy, so the IPs stayed busy. The jail was empty most of the time, but when there was a prisoner in there, we did check for any human rights violations. After conducting our checks, we traveled back to Al Asad. We were instructed to go to Hit, population 95,800. We traveled to Hit and stayed about three weeks, and we worked with the police station there. The police station was already established, so we conducted some training with the IPs and checked with the chief to see if he needed help with anything. We were instructed to go to Ramadi, population 192,556. We were not to meet with the police station, but we were to attend some high-profile meetings. After the meetings were adjourned, we went back to Hit, and I went back to Camp Mesa. My second year contract was over, and I was heading back home to Texas.

At Camp Mesa, I packed my bags to get ready to head back to Texas. For two years, I was at and able to help the communities in the cities and towns of Ar-Rutbah, Walid, Akashat, Al-Qaim, Romanah, Sadah, Rawa, Anah, Kha Al Baghdadi, and Hit. I do thank God that I was with our US Marines. I am very glad that I spent those two years helping the Sunni Muslim people. The Marines flew me from Al Asad to Baghdad, on the Osprey, and then I got a ride to Camp Klecher. If I only had a dollar for every time I had to cross the Euphrates River. I was then flown to Amman, Jordan, from where I headed to Dallas-Fort Worth. Anthony Marquez picked me up, and I was back in Texas.

# ISIS ENTERS MY CROSSHAIRS

When I got back into Fort Worth, I felt something was wrong with my head, but it was not PTSD. I gave it eight months, and my head still did not feel right. I thought moving to my home state of Montana for a while might help. I talked with Anthony and told him that I had moved away from home, in 1987, when I joined the Air Force, so it would be good to reconnect with my family and friends. Anthony thought I would be away for two years and that I would be back in Texas. I packed up my truck and headed back home to Billings, Montana.

Once I got back home, a friend from Texas, Robert Ramirez, came to Billings to visit with me and check on me. Robert and I were stationed in Germany together in 1995 as well as for the main push into Baghdad in 2003. I told him I needed time to clear my head. I wanted to let my hair grow out, put it in a ponytail, and get a job in a warehouse. We both laughed, and he headed back to Texas. I went to work for a security job with Securitas for a year and then with TSA for two years. After spending three years in Montana, my head was all clear. A friend of mine from Texas, Randy Thurman, came to Colstrip, Montana. We were together for the main push into Baghdad in 2003, and we had a good visit in Colstrip. He did ask me when I was coming back to Texas. I told him I didn't know but that I felt much better. He headed back to Texas. I got hold of Anthony and told him it had been three years and that I was ready to move back to Texas. I moved back to Texas.

In 2013, I went to work with Universal Protection Service, so I would find myself working security and fighting against ISIS. In 2014, ISIS took over Fallujah, Iraq, and our US military briefed President Barack Obama about the situation. He called ISIS a JV team. There would be no US boots on the ground in Iraq, and the United States and the coalition would conduct only air strikes. Obama wanted ISIS contained. ISIS also took over all of the cities and towns in the whole of Anbar Province of Iraq. All of our hard efforts and dedicated work were to no avail. In my own mind, I put ISIS in my crosshairs. I wanted ISIS fully out of Iraq and Syria and then completely off of this planet. I wondered how the IPs and communities were doing under ISIS rule, and I prayed to God that they are still alive. With Presidents Obama order of no boots on the ground, I am retired from the military. I don't have to follow that order.

Over that year, the world watched as ISIS went into high gear killing innocent people, both in Iraq and Syria. ISIS ratcheted up its own PR by recording their killings, shooting people, beheading people, and throwing people off of building roofs. It works as thousands are drawn to join the ISIS ranks. I remember when ISIS shot down the Jordan jet plane, and the pilot was burned alive in the cage. ISIS attacked Europe—in Paris, France, 137 people were killed; in Brussels, Belgium, thirty-five people were killed. The

ISIS killing rampage is nonstop. This ISIS terrorist group has to be stopped. Thousands of refugees are fleeing, for no one can live freely under ISIS rule.

I was watching a story on the news about two former US soldiers, Jordan Matson and Jeremy Woodard, who had joined with the YPG Army in Syria, and they were fighting against ISIS. I was thinking about how they got there so quickly and that they would need to be reinforced. Jordan and I became friends on Facebook, and I was informed of what to do. I caught a flight to Russia and then to Germany, where I spent three days. I then flew to northern Iraq, where the YPG Army housed me in a safe house. The safe house kept other foreign fighters from other countries, including Mario from Portugal and Danny from Britain. We all made a quick road trip to the Tigris River, which we crossed in a raft. On the other side, we were officially in Syria. I got there in February 2015, and we found a way to fight against ISIS on its own turf.

We did go to an YPG camp, where other foreign fighters were staying, and there were thirteen of us in our group from Iran, Russia, Spain, Canada, Portugal, Australia, Britain, the United States, and other places. We all went to the training academy, did some training, and were issued weapons and a uniform. We told the general that we were ready to fight ISIS. Danny from Britain, Brandon from Canada, and I were sent to the front line. The YPG Army is 50,000 strong, and it took very good care of us. We got three meals a day. We were sent to the Rojava area, which is north of Damascus. The day that we stepped foot on the battlefield, we witnessed the YPG Army start its offense against ISIS, and it did not let up. Some YPG soldiers on the ground were fighting ISIS as coalition jets above were bombing ISIS positions. During the four months I was fighting with YPG, it never let up on the ISIS positions.

For about a week, we had to clear out the villages that ISIS left behind, and from time to time, we could hear gunfire ahead, as the YPG kept pushing ISIS out of the area. We were then put with an YPG team. Our commander was twenty-four years old, and there were about twenty soldiers to the team. They were issued three white Toyota trucks to get around in on the battlefield, which we all had to pile into when we moved. As we moved to other advance positions, we had to fortify the position. We would fill sandbags using big bulldozer and set up round-the-clock security to make sure ISIS did not come back at us while we slept. We couldn't talk with YPG directly, but as time went on, we all did laugh and point. We became friends, and they liked to dance, sing, cook, play games, drink chia three times a day, look at family pictures, and take pictures.

We were briefed that we will be moving closer to the front. Conditions were very dangerous. We loaded our bags and weapons into our trucks. Once our relief got there, we moved out and drove for a long time. I witnessed empty homes, entire communities left behind, for no one wants to live under ISIS rule. They all had fled to Europe. We made it to our next position, and some of our guys were there already. They pointed to where the ISIS position is, which is right in the next town. They take us to the security point, and you can clearly see ISIS walking around. I figured they were about two football fields away. I used the binoculars and could see the black flag waving around on top of the town building, I couldn't wait for this moment—I wanted to go kill the bastards. We went inside, and Danny had to go to the bathroom. A bullet went flying over his head, so he came running back inside. I was issued only one uniform, and trying to keep that clean was impossible. We did not take full showers. It took hours just to heat up the water. All we could do was wash up as best we could. We shaved and cut hair as best as we could. Some of the guys ended up just growing a full beard, but you just can't get rid of that stink.

We got into a habit of taking potshots at ISIS. One day, Danny and I were potshots at ISIS, and we heard a big boom. Something went flying over our heads, and we looked at each other and asked what that had been. Some of the YPG guys came out, looked around, and told us that ISIS had just lobbed a mortar round over our heads. The round went way back, so no one got hurt. About three times a week, we got into small scrimmages with ISIS, and our coalition jets would drop bombs on its position, and we could see black smoke rise into the air. At night, when we had fires going and were dancing and singing, bullets would go flying over our heads. When we first got there, our team was split up into two groups, covering two positions on the town. There was a road that separated our two positions. A few weeks later, I was separated from Danny and Brandon and was sent with the other group. Of course, we still kept up with the small scrimmage with ISIS from there.

It was the last week of May. The three of us, Danny, Brandon, and I, had been fighting alongside the YPG Army. At about midnight, we fired every weapon we had into the ISIS position for two and half hours. We even fired mortars. We ran low on ammo, the guys went and got more, and I helped distribute to whoever needed it. Danny and Brandon said they fired everything they had, for they thought that ISIS might over flank us and overrun their position. At about three that morning, we stopped firing and went to bed. The next morning, I had the security point, and when the sun came up, I counted ten of its buildings on fire. I was told we had killed about thirteen ISIS terrorists. About a week later, one of the YPG generals came around, and I was told that I would be sent back home. I asked if that meant back to Texas, and they said yes. I told them thanks, but I wanted to stay until July, because that would give me six months. I was told that Danny and Brandon were being sent back home, and I was told I would be leaving with them. I said, "Yes, sir." I said goodbye to my YPG Army friends and wished them well with the fight against ISIS.

When I got back to the safe house in Iraq, I sent Anthony an email asking him to pick me up at the airport. Anthony picked me up in my truck. I put my bag away in the back, and I got into the front passenger seat. As we started driving down the road, he said, "You stink."

I told him, "Yeah, I know. Sorry. Is Whataburger open?"

I was planning on going back in September 2016, but we were informed that the Syrian government had closed the border between Syria and Iraq, so we couldn't cross the Tigris River to join back up with the YPG Army. I do thank God that I was able to help the Kurdish Muslim people.

34

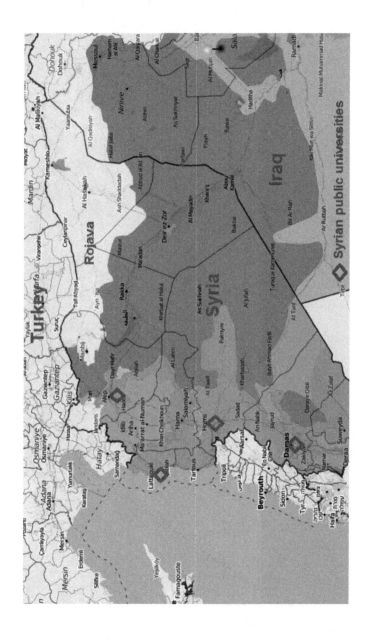

Printed in the United States
By Bookmasters